D1581012

Ewald Murrer

THE DIARY
of
MR. PINKE

translated by Alicie Pišťková

TWISTED SPOON PRESS
Prague

This book is sponsored by
John Bruce Shoemaker
and restaurant Derby

ISBN: 80-90-1257-4-3

Translator's Note

In some cases the first person is referred to in the third person which was a common form of addressing oneself in the Hasidic Jewish villages of Galicia. I have attempted to maintain this distinction in hopes of capturing some of the formality. Under the heading »October 22« there occurs a reference to the Czech proverb, »Don't buy rabbits in a bag,« meaning you should not buy what you cannot see. Rather than substitute a rough English equivalent, and to keep the flavor of the text, I have translated this literally.

I would like to thank Lucie Pistek for helping me find the proper words, Vladímira Žáková for taking the time to go over the Czech text, and Amy R. Nestor and Howard Sidenberg for their energy and thoroughness in editing the manuscript.

No one went
and still
only the sound
of the song's wind.

I went to the forest behind Isaac Antan's estate.

In the forest, trees leaned toward my face. Branches entirely covered my body, they twined like arms around me.

Suddenly, I saw myself in the dimmest gorge in the rocks.

Then, toward evening, the embrace loosened; I quietly gave them my regards, and left.

It will be
beautiful when
the lights go out.

Today Mr. Chaim Finkel came from Prague. I waited for him at the station. Our station is only a small depot. It is far from Voronskie Put'.

From the high steps of the train, Mr. Finkel descended heavily.

He was completely worn out.

The train departed and we stood alone in the fog. A fog that enveloped all but the station building, the pigsties next to it, a pump, and a couple of crones in black, who watched us with tiny, staring eyes.

Finkel grasped the handle of the suitcase and we set off for the house.

On the way, Finkel wanted to say something, but a huge tangle of fog covered us, crept into our lungs, and sealed our eyes. Finkel wiped his with a buckskin glove. The crones in black had vanished. The fog was thick. Even the depot had vanished. Finkel wanted to know where he would sleep and where he would eat.

The fog dispersed, the carriage carried us to the village. I escorted Mr. Chaim Finkel into the house.

If the clock has struck,
take the key
and open the trunk.

Yesterday I put up Mr. Chaim Finkel from Prague. Mr. Chaim Finkel from Prague is a businessman. He has come to purchase some land on which the company Isaac Meisel wants to build small factories for processing sheep's wool.

»It won't work out,« I told him.

In the evening, he drank liquor.

Outside, all day, there was fog.

Finkel did not once leave the house.

*Death tickling
round my mouth.*

Today Finkel was taken by the house. I showed him around, through the cellar and the attic.

My house is without windows, made of stone, with walls up to seven feet thick. He wondered, why without windows. I answered: »The region here, beasts, werewolves, dwarves – better without windows.«

Rooster on the tower,
why do you spin?

Still fog.

Mr. Finkel, the rabbi, and I walked around. Thick fog. Damp.

Finkel wanted to have the carriage harnessed. Coachman Rabrath was nowhere to be found. I looked for him in the house. In the cellar, the attic.

The rabbi waved his hand, »Forget Rabrath.«

»We'll get nowhere on foot,« said Finkel.

»We won't,« said I.

The rabbi waved his hand. A big tangle of fog began to close in on us. The rabbi grabbed Finkel, stood with his back to the approaching fog and when it reached us, lay down on it. He dragged Finkel down with him. I, too, jumped onto the fog.

We flew away from the village. Finkel was amazed at the soft comfort of the fog.

After a while the village became faint.

Do you toll
alarm?
I do not toll
this way.

Still fog.

The dog roamed about, then brought an owl from the forest. At the table Finkle grumbled –

»What a strange land, you're afraid that you'll trip over a dwarf, that the neighbor at the table in the tavern is a werewolf, that – I don't know what else.«

– »I, too, don't know what else,« I said.

The owl had emerald eyes.

*The crack in
the door glanced
slyly at me.*

I leaned on the stone railing of the footbridge, thinking aloud. On the railing, a seagull alighted.

I was thinking about ghosts.

»Surely you wouldn't believe in ghosts,« said the seagull.

»He almost would,« I replied.

Then I realized he was a seagull and said:

»It is you who speaks to me, I am surprised, seagull.«

»Don't be surprised, Pinke,« he said.

»And don't be afraid,« he added.

»I had been thinking of ghosts,« I said.

»I am not a ghost,« said the seagull.

»You know, I still haven't got used to you talking,« I said.

»Don't worry Pinke, after all, I, too, was once unable to get used to people talking to me – so don't be afraid, I don't bite.«

APRIL 1

*In the palms
the pitcher
maliciously yawned.*

At night I took the forest trail from Stolové to Pluzhno.

I had to change my round glasses for the square ones.

Now, close to morning, I change the square for the round.

Dawn.

The peasant goes home,
the soup smells
of village.

In my life I have come to know merely seven gardens and six cities. The rest is as if in a fog. I only passed through.

Seven gardens and six cities. Sultry, languid noon, branches of the alders. Stairs already cold. Fractured midnight.

Most likely the time before the Last Judgement.

Dawn gazing upward, a timid rooster transports the astronomer along the flames. A swan is the wind.

Shortly before judgement.

Harpies haunt the stairs,
Furies scratch the door.
We tremble in corners.

Have you ever considered what spiders, locked in dark rooms where no fly ever enters, where not a single strand of light ever falls, feed on? Where only the dim light of a glowing candle casts sporadic shadows on a cracked wall?

Have you noticed how many hands the spider has empty?

Isaac Antan looked through the door into my house. He pressed his face against the glass pane. He said nothing and left again.

Isaac Antan is our richest man, he is rich like no other here, like few anywhere. He is mute.

I often see him in the woods. By the meadows where deer go. His eyes are the same as theirs, and his lips are always moist.

The Gypsy Dilmatsch speaks to him with glances. Antan smiles at him. Dilmatsch is our poorest.

Dilmatsch brought me a violin to fix. It had burst.

You shall leave
and a dog shall follow
to lick the drops
which manage
to escape you.

A visit to my friend Mumelschau. Mumelschau is an old, black, very horned goat. He is a crazy old fool. And he drinks liquor. He has a famous tomcat, Elem Ryschon. The Elem Ryschon who lies behind the stove in my house.

Ryschon is black, furry, and covered with silver spots – with little stars. Mumelschau gazes dreamily at Elem Ryschon; he sends him for liquor. Elem goes willingly. Mumelschau then hangs silver charms on his fleece.

For the goat king they
on two fingers played.

Old Gypsy Dilmatsch went to the seer. The seer
lives in Lesná at Pluzhno. Old Gypsy Dilmatsch
has had a premonition. He sees images on the wall
at home. On his shabby wall he sees magnificent
paintings by the masters. Magnificent, smiling
baroque figures.

Tomorrow old Dilmatsch will come for the violin
he brought to me burst.

»We are immortal, we will never die,«
said my uncle.
I was sitting in his lap,
still quite small and mortal.

Cloves of garlic hang on the windowframe.

Outside, the round moon. The dog has fallen asleep. Across the road, old Kascheljaková was airing the feather beds.

At night it snowed a little, unusual.

Today a heavy cart, dragged by three pairs of horses, arrived, carrying a bell.

Wipe
the scythe,
run
down the hill.

I daily observe such a story, although I am not actually aware of it. The forest is scented, the Sun lays it down like fresh fish on a stove. Darkness comes.

The Moon squabbles with the Sun about the fish on the stove. Darkness thickens, the Moon chases away the Sun, turns over the fish, and everything begins again from the opposite end.

I shall keep
but the shroud's shred
in remembrance.

In the morning the river hurled the fish onto the bank.

I went out.

The road up the hill is lined with aspens.

Dwarves, sitting in the trees, toss down leaves, make autumn under my feet. The leaves are sered from the heat.

Then I noticed that those malicious dwarves did this, that I might better hear the footsteps of the dogs about me.

What is an escape
to who knows where?

Damp in the cellar. Rats scurry around.

Walls like the bodies of old men, chased far away, out of sight. The damp stones of the walls were like the tortured bodies of pilgrims. Only a little sadness in the corners, and a thousand moldy tears, sighs. The fate of rats.

I sat on a three-legged stool, as I sometimes do in the cellar, and conversed with the stones.

In the corner was Mr. Finkel's leather suitcase. That sad businessman had left it here.

Into the fiery throat
of Moloch
we slid with ease.

I reminisced in a silence made for reminiscing.

I remembered how, when young, I went to school. During choir I would hit myself on the nose with a ruler, until I bled.

Then I would stand by the sink and wash myself. I liked water, not choir.

Today a postal-card came from Mr. Murrer from Vršovice. Bad news, Count von Fisch – again.

Steps in the belfry, creaking
– Grim Reaper, come to us.
And the old bell-ringer will just not die.

I drove off to Pluzhno. I put a leather bag of garlic in my pocket, then some paper bags with cloves, horsetail, sage, and belladonna.

An enormous paper horse was on display on the square in Pluzhno. He was colorfully painted and smiling happily. He was hollow, and his back had already burst.

Children were screaming like small, obstinate monkeys.

Stands with wares.

I bought something.

Off a corner of the square, on Jakubská street, a new photographer's studio.

On our way –
one day,
two days –
there by dusk.
Jerusalem at dawn,
tomorrow we go.

Old Kascheljaková brought an amazing treasure from the Pluzhno market. She showed it to me, bound by oath, today. It was wrapped in silk – a horn of the mythical unicorn. My dreamed-of hoofed creature.

I asked about the merchant who sold it. An unknown foreign Jew. Black as coal.

Gendarme Weissbaum sang in the liquor store. He sat in his uniform like a farmer. He was not on duty. I was asking about Pluzhno – he knows everything about the market. He even knows many numbers.

He knows the Jew with the coal-like face. He knows him well, he'll send for him.

In my dreams, the unicorn gallops. Hooves clattering. The horn shining spectacularly.

My carriage
tears quickly along,
a long time has passed
since the horses last bolted.

It was cozy in the tiny tavern, lit with candles. In the corner slept the old Gypsy Dilmatsch.

Innkeeper Bem, myself, and shopkeeper Kornilov were conversing, as usual, about the village.

Mr. Bem was apprehensive about farmer Kleinitsch's health; for the third day now, he has not come home. Agitated, shopkeeper Kornilov put his hand on Mr. Bem's arm, saying that Kleinitsch was surely a werewolf. Mr. Bem crossed himself. Kornilov recounted a meeting with Kleinitsch the night before in the forest above Orlovka.

The owls were hooting more than usual; old Gypsy Dilmatsch turned and spoke in his sleep.

Mr. Bem left for liquor. Kornilov confusedly told me about portends in the sky. It seems to be a time of evil powers

The door opened, the gendarme entered – he drank a glass of liquor.

Apparently, Kleinitsch had been found strangled by a wolf.

Old Gypsy Dilmatsch fell under the table.

*The wind embraced
me with a smile.*

Elem Ryschon awakened me; he jumped onto my
face, then growled apologetically, looked furtively
around, and cleaned his coat.

I got up abruptly. The meeting had been set for
three in the morning. The meeting with Mr. Smurny.

Fog.

I hooted into the window and a bat darted out; he
gave a long squeal and disappeared beyond the
horizon.

Later they told me he had flown north.

Then, in the windows, the heads of Smurny's
children could be seen. Six girls. Black-haired dolls.
Light flashed on the walls. Barúch Smurny descended
with a torch.

We went across the field. The moss-covered
dome, cold and indifferent, did not welcome us.

We entered. Under the roof there is a spring. We
cleaned it quickly, without words.

The past does not return,
it runs along the present.
A mask on its face.

    In the cave I carelessly touched a bat; he was cold and for a long time I heard his shrill swaying.

As I close my eyes at night,
I send thoughts to the houses.
With aching arms
and aching tongue,
I chase sinful lambs.

Mr. Fuks came.

Mr. Fuks is Jewish, black as coal. He came with a cart and a donkey. He brought ten horns of the fabled unicorn. All real. I caressed them. Mr. Fuks did not say where he acquired them. He smiled mysteriously. He is a businessman.

He came from faraway. A very capable businessman. An adventurer, however. He spoke of many interesting things. Then, from out of his cart, he produced wolf heads, crow wings, mare tails, horns of goats, cow horns, several hooves, and hides.

He is also a scientist, he knows nature well.

He catches birds with lime.

He weaves cages.

Are bats more stony
than our garden?

I went to Pluzhno to the post office. A couple of letters in my pocket. I am writing to Mr. Murrer in Vršovice. Mr. Murrer likes stories from our region; I like pleasing him with them.

I am also writing to Duke Erich in Warsaw. Duke Erich struts around in red fox fur. He is a hunter. He chases game in the parks. Even in Greenland, there he hunted silver foxes. Their hides hung in Warsaw, in the shop window of furrier Frankl. One thousand zloty a pair. Women like wearing silver fur. The duke, red.

I also wrote to Preschov, to landowner Kolmatchek. Landowner Kolmatchek is newly-wed, he has Janka for a wife. He is a poet. He hosts artists; they drink Hungarian wine.

On horses, moths sit.
With birds, the sky darkened.

Kornilov brought two crystalline bottles of liquor. We drank it with fish. Kornilov enjoys speaking about ominous signs. He observes them in the sky. The midnight stars say fascinating things. They know the whole village and talk about it. And they even know whole cities. Among them – Prague, also Uzhgorod, Warsaw, and Berlin.

Kornilov carries a map in his pocket. The map, too, is full of stars, it is an astrological map. Full of numbers, full of endless zeroes.

Kornilov is a shopkeeper. He includes fortune-telling among his wares. He doesn't charge for fortunetelling. He wraps the goods in the *KrähePuter Blatt*.

Here it is appropriate to mention the interesting figure of the editor, Süsser. I meet with him sometimes. Abel Süsser publishes the village paper, *KrähePuter Blatt*. Sometimes I read it.

The scythes are sharpened,
let's fling ourselves
at their feet!

Today the wind caught me by the hand and led me out of the village. It led me through the fields. Night descended. The village lit up behind me. Fires burning, birds flying, calling something to one another.

I went along the road, breathed the aroma of the ears of grain, looked forward to returning to the village from which I had just come, smiled happily.

Then a horse appeared on the horizon. On his back he carried a proud figure. Gendarme Weissbaum was riding somewhere. The saber swayed along the horse's body.

So many grains perished
in the storm,
even the bread soggy
in the peasants' palms.

With a loud creak I opened the door. A strange bird took off and flew, slowly and unsteadily, away. The orphaned branch wailed. The bird shrieked and returned. He sat down again and straightened his grey feathers.

I put on high boots; I walked in damp grass.

An ordinary early morning.

I am other
than I would have been,
had I known myself
before I was born.

I experienced fear.

Our region lends itself to fear.

It lends itself to incidents. I saw a phantom, it resembled something, most likely a wolf. Something like a wolf, something large, vague, but horrible, uncanny.

When I noticed the grey phantom standing quietly and menacingly like a ruined house, I became unspeakably terrified, took a step back, sat down, and burst out crying.

I sat on a stone with an imprint of a human foot. I had to say aloud, »Only a human foot.«

We left together,
just like before.

I lit the oil lamp. A big moth rocked on the wall, dazzled by the light, and fell into the plate of aspic. Blubbering and whining.

Outside an incorporeal cloud, resembling a corpse, strode by.

I was you –
and you were me.

Again, today, I met the landowner in the forest clearing above Orlovka. He was staring at deer. I did not disturb him.

A little further off, old Gypsy Dilmatsch was sleeping in the undergrowth. My footsteps awoke him. He put his finger to his lips and again closed his eyes.

A large cat, prying, walked by. It sized us up with a cold look.

A sudden gust of wind howled, »Corpse, corpse.«

At night, in the tavern, landowner Antan sat with the groom Shalom Nagad. They had moist lips.

The rabbi was shuffling tarot cards.

Sad fields,
birds' eyes.

Today, a happy day. Mr. Murrer arrived unannounced, suddenly. An automobile bounced laboriously along our deep road.

He quickly knocked on the door.

We went; on the village square an old woman stopped us.

»You are messengers of royal foolishness,« she said.

»You are knights – messengers,« she said.

Then, at night, we lit a large fire in the meadow of Mumelschau the goat. A good deal of liquor was put away and some chickens, also an abundance of fish.

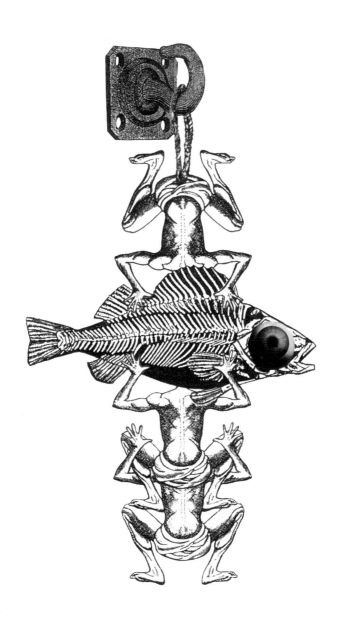

The wind turned
us inside out,
dry flowers fell
from our pockets.

Murrer sat at the table reading a massive leather-bound book. He was reading aloud; it was my book. I fed the fire and quietly it spoke.

Birds squeezed
into traps –
open arms.

    Mr. Murrer again sat at the table. He was reading my other book bound in pigskin.

*Under the sod
snakes lie.*

Mr. Ewald Murrer left. At midday, without saying a word, he started up his vehicle and quickly set off on his uncomfortable journey.

He forgot his suitcase of fine pigskin. I carried it into the cellar, placed it next to the suitcase of Mr. Finkel.

Then I sat on the three-legged stool and had a long conversation with the wall.

Afterward, upstairs, I portioned a fish, ate half and left half on the plate. I even divided the bread.

The automobile left deep tracks in the earth.

Fingers are pegs
for violins,
palms are the bridge,
wobbly from singing.

At two in the afternoon a wooden wagon drove behind the village. It drove alone, without a team, unhitched. It drove for a while along the horizon. We watched it, Dilmatsch, Bem, Weissbaum, Nagad, Potok, Elem Ryschon, and I.

Potok then went to the spot where the wagon was stuck in a thicket. He went with a whip and exhorted the wagon on. But the wagon no longer wanted to drive alone. Dilmatsch ran to the Potoks' for horses. He brought back a dapple-grey one.

Meteors in the sky.

They fell into the pond behind Orlovka.

The eyes of the rabbi,
flew off to the fields,
doves.
　　　　(Yom Kever)

Behind the village, Saul Potok was constructing a brick building.

Behind the construction, black kids with white hooves were walking. At night the moon took them into the heavens. Their hooves were stars.

White kids also graze there. They graze in the morning.

Milk runs down the hills.

In the fire
shepherds
roast potatoes.

I met Shalom Nagad, the groom. He stood on the edge of the field. We then ran through the deep road.

We rushed to the horizon.

We sat on the horizon. Dogs from the village greeted us. Red dusk lit the sky.

A woman stood in the distance. She was picking apples from low branches.

In the copse, a black goblin slurped red wine.

He grimaced countless ways. Then he clenched his neck with a claw and strangled his body. He fell to the grass hissing. He evaporated into the seeds of the trees.

At morning he blossomed into a black flower laced with red veins.

A hungry roebuck in these areas.

The queen died slowly,
she was cruel and surly.

Tonight, I cannot sleep; nor will I even sleep tomorrow, toward morning. I went further away from home. I greeted the marsh.

Here in the blackness, a secret flower blossoms at midnight. A beautiful, enormous white flower.

It attracts quiet bats.

The dank mud reeked of spices.

A metallic night
and extinguished lights.

Saul Potok was planting trees by his brick house, oaks. He dug the pits with a bluish spade.

I sat on the rocks as he did. He ate bread. Spoke little. The goat wandered over to us, drank wine from a bellows.

Then they brought a letter from Mr. Murrer from Prague. Count von Fisch, some troubles with Carmen.

Leave the mute
silent,
let the deaf
listen.

A night of strange eyes and cat shrieks.

Tree torsos. . .

When I walk through the night, my steps ring like a song, monotonously, in rhythm with the road.

When I walk through the night, my legs sing a solitary song, a song of furtive glances.

Shadows accompany me.

Shadowy kisses, touches, and scuffles.

In the morning we took the britzska to Orlovka. Gloom in Müllberger's pottery shop. The purring wheel. In my palms I kneaded the clay. He was creating unwittingly an absent-minded demiurge.

Müllberger worked in silence, master of the potter's wheels.

Which animal
do you like?
The animal that
runs in the distance.

The face of the landscape, overgrown by high weeds, cracked and dusty, is not a privilege of Voronskie alone. It is the look of a landscape scrupulously guarded by dwarves, werewolves, wizards, winged animals, and ghouls.

How to describe a bird in flight if it were to be important for the event of a day? Dark sky, fast flying birds, hurriedly flapping their wings. Then a swarm of rocks flying upward.

The banquet begins,
the eating of raw meat.

I lure goblins with words. First came the she-goblins of the under-leaves, small grave diggers, coffins, full of dead leaves, in hand. Hands soft as kittens. Blackish goblins with rakes and brooms and baskets.

Then sad he-goblins flew in the wind, their arms waving, wailing.

In the evening tell yourself something,
so as to not fall asleep all night.

»Mr. Pinke, Mr. Pinke! – look, he says that my dogs must be sad!«

Gypsy Dilmatsch was calling after me. »He says that my dogs must, must be sad!« He pointed to the tiny rag-merchant Saul Blumensee.

»But my dogs, Mr. Pinke, my dogs can't be sad!« Dilmatsch was close to tears. »My dogs are unable to be sad!« He took his violin out of his knapsack and played. He ran from us playing. The dogs swirled around him, barking.

It was already growing dark, the peasants were returning from the fields, behind the village, the wispy bodies of ancestors fluttered. And among all this grandeur, dogs and violins were laughing.

He swung a silk cord
Grains of dust huddled closer together
A beak cleaning the rooster's tail
Claws clenching a branch.

Today Mr. Murrer celebrated the day of his birth. He arrived early in the morning with his friend Yom Kever. A full car for the celebration.

Again, many breams were consumed. A bouquet of pansies filled the house with an unpleasant odor. I got up and threw it out the door. Elem Ryschon brought Mumelschau. Mumelschau drank liquor and let out a long, sad bleat.

Yom Kever painted a picture on the wall.

He pressed his face
to the light.

A stone footbridge fell in the forest.

The gentlemen Murrer and Kever walked for some
time in the graveyard. Perhaps they even peered into
the open graves.

I cleaned the pigeon loft.

He prepared for the journey.

I call into the chimney.

    We drove off to Pluzhno by car, Mr. Yom Kever at the wheel. I stopped in at the post office to see Berka the postmaster. The gentlemen walked through the attics, through the cellars. They even glanced at the pigsties.

Dear Count!

This letter, sir, concerns your land behind the forest at Voronskie Puť. It is rumored, sir, that at one time your father mined silver on this land. You, then, as you know yourself, to the astonishment of the whole domain, stopped the mining and, with that, drove your miners into indigence and insecurity. Sir, I do not wish to reproach you for a thing, come to terms with your soul yourself. However, sir, I would like to point out that queer things are happening there in the forest. Many lights are ablaze there at midnight, and the souls of the dead are mining. The spirit of your dear father, supposedly with his head in his hand, weeps haltingly between the funeral candles. As a good son, sir, you should do something to save his suffering spirit.

Yours,
Elházár Rischonel, Jr.

This letter, which postmaster Berka found sunken in the office files, had lain there lost for sixty years, and Mr. Berka gave it to me seeing that neither the Count nor Mr. E. Rischonel, the rug-maker, is alive, and Mr. Berka knows me as a collector of oddities from our region.

I gave the letter to Mr. Murrer; I think he, too, is interested in such stories.

Excuse me,
death is standing
behind the door,
do you want to see it?

The gentlemen Kever and Murrer are leaving. A banquet. We baked pig-snouts.

Yom Kever hung fish on the trees. He cut pretty paper decorations. He cleaned the fireplace with a birch broom.

Then, in a procession, we went to the castle – in front, Mr. Murrer, I , then half the village – Dilmatsch, Kornilov, Bem, Kascheljak, Rabrath, Smurny, Jacob, gendarme Weissbaum, Süsser, Nagad, and then, at the end, Kever, and in the distance, Ryschon and Mumelschau.

At the castle, windows boarded up, a smell of chlorine. We went far behind Voronskie Puť, almost to Orlovka; Süsser had his shoes hanging from his shoulder. Dilmatsch had none.

Above Orlovka a herd of wild boars ran listlessly by us. Ryschon caught a bird.

Soft canine glances,
my midnight tracks.

A pernicious breed of mice flooded the region. The bare fields teemed with their tiny bodies. If someone had observed them, he would have seen their life to be surrounded by severity, enveloped in a peculiar spirit, a regularity of striking intention. The mice ran along strictly defined paths. It seemed they avoided one another, because no one ever spotted them running the well-trodden path together, not even in twos. Their life recalled the life of some strange order of monks.

Mr. Isaac Antan, a small man whose sparse, spiky whiskers jutted out, watched the piles in the granaries with apprehension. The wheat disappearing before his eyes.

The piles throbbed, changed shape, and toppled as the mouse thieves, not understanding their misdemeanor, gnawed away in their entrails.

The stablehands were assigned the task of destroying the unwelcome and repeatedly cursed guests.

With clubs and knives they ran through the granaries and fields. Mouse corpses were heaped up in incredible numbers across the entire village.

Even Shalom Nagad, Mr. Antan's groom, took a knife and went out to do murder. In a granary, an inexplicable terror gripped him. He fell to his knees and beseeched god for the generation of slain mice. He could not even lift the knife to deliver the death blow. He spoke to the mice and apologized before them for his fellow stablemates.

He filled the bag designated for the corpses with live mice. Each one, individually, he begged not to think ill of Shalom Nagad, and he feared to meet the eyes of any one of them.

With his bag full of mice, he started across the field to his house. On the way he was unusually, involuntarily happy.

He even caught solitary, monkish field mice and thew them in with the fat, worldly granary mice.

At home he untied the bag and the mice ran out, all of a sudden there was even less room than before, wherever the eye fell sat one of those strange forms.

»David,« they called Nagad.

Look, the goblins are fleeing on snake feet.
Seizing the keg, their king leaves through the cellar.

Peasants caught a red snake in the fields. They clubbed him in a fierce battle.

A catfish mouth peers out from the pond.

Children run through the village and loudly shout – »He's scared of mice, he's scared of mice!« They shout at Mr. Nagad. Mr. Nagad, their amusement. They run after him.

He really is afraid of mice and no child even knows why.

To each what is good –
Half the kingdom,
Rags, bones, old junk,
dishes, pewter pots, scratched plaster,
bricks, raven carrion,
half a lunch.

Brides descended from the hills. There, in the hills,
they have a custom of holding weddings by the dozen.
Twelve brides went. A herd of decorated kids,
groomed cows. An old, melancholy horse with a cart.

And they carried long tables out to the roads.

At the crossroads, wild music.

*Here and there they hid
in the courtyard.*

You could see the garden. We stood with
Kascheljak in his house, by the window. He was
caressing the tree branches. Then they brought an
axe from the attic. We left the house.

When the tree fell, I found a book in its roots. We
examined the trunk as a doctor a wound.

At night, chilly in the feather bed, a woodworm
moving the bookcase.

Affix rose lattice
to the cities.

Meteors flew across the sky again.

Foxes in the country, wolves in the villages.

I sat at home on a chair and looked at the table. If I had gotten up, I would have reached for a cane and beaten the table. I did not get up.

Snakes crawling into holes.

Foreboding.

The cold days I'll cover
up with my hands.

The merchant Fuks drove in donkeys. He sold them for cheap to the farmers. Even I bought a donkey cheaply. Then I sent for Elem Ryschon and for Mumelschau the goat, and we welcomed the donkey.

The goat made inquiries. Then we thought up a name. Ryschon had an idea, first he hugged the donkey, kissed it. »You are Shalem,« he told him.

Return David,
I don't drive you out.
Don't be angry with me,
that I am your enemy.

Moths frantically attacked the candle. They could not wait to touch it. From the cold to the blaze. To awaken. I flee the cold, willing to yield to crazed thoughts.

Dog skulls in the shed, firewood for heating.

An angel fell from heaven.

I stood in the village square. Weissbaum and Bem stood there too.

Dilmatsch came to the square, crying. He walked with the sad violin without strings.

I said – »Don't cry.«

But he cried and pointed to the violin that did not have even one string, that could not play.

Then Weissbaum moved his arm and grabbed the violin and threw it into jail.

Into the black hole, let it fiddle there.

Fear watching
from afar.

Greenish lights in the fields. Fluid earth in the forests.

A dreadful thunderstorm in the early evening.

   Birds beaten in flight.

A walking cane lies abandoned behind the village.

   The storm left legible letters in the clouds, and then an entire hand, as if human.

The clock sleeps,
the wind ceased.
Night,
become day,
let all be
lost in light.

An odd thing happened to the house.

On the walls I noticed stumps of chicken wings, like sprouting mushrooms. Live, quivering in the stones.

I could feel blood circulating through the house, arteries growing into the walls to prevent any terrified brick, coaxed by the wind into flight, from escaping. So that not even smoke from the stove might take flight.

Perhaps even the soot grew into the walls, for the chimney sweep climbed out of the chimney, deaf with exhaustion, completely white. Without a word he walked across the field, stumbling to his knees, and never returned. He left his equipment behind, scattered on the doorstep.

Even his eyes are eternal.

A letter from Count von Fisch:

All which must be. And which questions are posed and how much is answered. And all which is not. And will not be.

How hard it is to begin a sentence, to start one's speech, without dramatically running one's fingers through one's hair, without coughing.

I have an open window behind my back and the wind is stroking my neck.

Here.

And there, far away, stands the castle, the house of hewed logs, which grew under the hands of an ancient people. That place, stolen from the forests.

The house and the garden, trees closed behind a high wall. Trees that have only one possibility of escape. No one forbade them an exit through the decorated gate. Just as no one forbade me an entrance there.

No one said you may not enter, your shoes may not damage the raked sand on the road to the castle. However, I am well aware that the staircase will carry my steps and the doorknob will yield under my hand and open the door without protest.

It is dark there, night, closed windows. A decorated coat of arms in grating, darkened by time.

*Wagon wheels
in a deep road.*

Foreign musicians showed up. They came for the night and played no songs. They wanted a place to sleep. They asked at Nagad's.

Shalom told them: »My dear sirs, you cannot sleep here with those violins, something here haunts every musician, tormenting unease will grip you here, who knows what kind of hell-hound is here, who knows why he doesn't let musicians rest.«

Then he nodded and let the foreign musicians into the hayloft.

»What did he say, Joseph?« said one.

»What do I know!« said the other.

»Watch out for our fiddles, let's gently lay them in the hay,« they both said. Then I still heard:

»How soft the hay is.«

»Well, good night.«

»'Night.«

With hands clenched,
with veins hardened.

Wooden argosies afloat in the clouds. An imminent thunderstorm. Only drizzle.

Large wooden vessels with sturdy masts rocking long in the distance. On deck, opaque animal contours. I observed the lively hustle and bustle. The throwing of ropes, anchors ornamented like chandeliers falling to earth.

I took a walk behind the village. Red birds sat by the pond. Their eyes were white, without pupils, without irises. The blind eyes of birds.

A rainy day
wet with tears.

Again a storm.

And again I sat in the wagon, smoking a cigarette. Next to me rode farmer Jacob and Elem Ryschon was sitting on my knees.

In Pluzhno I first visited the photographer's salon on Jakubská street. He stole my face.

Then I came to Hotel Hirsch and paid for the night.

In the evening I caught sight of my face in the window, after all. Suddenly, the glass in the window was surrounded by houses and the window was turning into a square. A square with a fountain. The fountain – that was my face.

And the houses were preening themselves, glancing in the mirror of the fountain.

Then, later in the evening, a bird alit on the window, wet himself in the fountain and, in surprise, splattered drops on my hands behind the glass.

And even later, mice moved the coat in the closet and moths moved their wings.

Forests grown silent,
trees quiet,
their voice other,
than it was.

Once more, a fierce rain sprang up. Pluzhno became dark. The rain water played on the house-drums wildly. Even passers-by were unmercifully hammered, even the cat behind the chimney.

I laughed out loud. Then the sun broke through a cloud. After all, that light is yours, so low above the ground.

Elem Ryschon came wet from town.

Aching feet
breath hard to catch,
from running on the horizon.

The road was long, it ran before me; when I was just able to grasp it by the coat, it disappeared beyond the horizon. It showed me its face from a distance.

I am invited to a fire this evening. I won't go.

The fire actually burned at night. Several houses burnt down as well.

I am running to the marshes
stripped of my skin.

    Still on the roads in the surroundings, I didn't sleep at home. I haven't slept at all for two nights. The house is like a burning oven, impossible to enter.

    A rat ran from the old rock cross, crying. Then its paws twitched and it died at my feet. I stood over it for a while.

    The road, dust, dryness, a feeling of something.

A cricket burst out in a sinister laugh.

The jerky movements of the clouds threw bones of fear upon me.

I craved a glimpse of what was beyond the horizon. I walked along a road lined with dinosaur skeletons.

    I have abandoned my Garden; unsteadily, I fumble along.

    Then I sat in the tavern in Orlovka. One of the better in town. Again, they invited me to the fire. I was drinking wine.

Life begins in the pistils,
we collect the spider's
broken legs.

The road brought me to a tavern. I saw only unfriendly faces there. There was silence and everyone ran off when I wanted to talk. Those that did not run off, they laughed and censured me.

A wheel in my head.

I listened to those unfriendly faces, and I heard sympathy.

Flowers in the gardens, trees in the forests understand me; I am understood by violins, strings as well as woodwinds, nay – the percussion understand me.

I got up and left.

Dilmatsch was walking across the village square with his violin. It was obvious, even from a distance, that it understood me.

With her palm she caressed
the annual rings of my soul.

I am the pilgrim of a small region. The region has solid borders that I cannot cross.

Every morning I leave, awakened by the singing of the birds or by the bell in the tree towers or by the voice of someone who is an awakener. I leave by the road which runs along the wall of blue stones. I leave secretly through the wall of my determined existence. I leave the door closed to cover the emptiness I hide.

I love colored rocks.

Sometimes, I go as an ascetic, in a borrowed suit.

At night I return. I am welcomed by the canine understanding of the quiet darkness, which also leaves in the morning without looking around.

Pilgrimage to a remote hill
where a stone tower
and a rare tree.

On the threshold I began to wander through the house. Aaron Jacob greeted me with his black eyes. From the table, the aromatic smell of simple food.

We went on a long journey amidst the house, counting the stairs, the doors raspingly laughing.

With the hand's key we overpowered the locks. With the hand's book we conquered the upper and lower floors, the depths, the heights.

The halls fragrant with soap, footsteps fading into the cracks.

Then, with a soft handle, a door stopped us. Completely covered with the prints of a child's hand. And on the window stood flowerpots, full of dry trees. Cobwebs waving in the cold wind.

Aaron carried wood for the fire.

By the ceiling hung a wooden bird, lord of the drafts, messenger of the distant winds.

A star will appear
and it will speak.

At night the door was shaking, I got up and opened it.

Outside, a beautiful unicorn with a rein on its neck and a bit. Even more, it was outfitted with a splendidly embroidered saddle.

I grasped the bit and – grasped nothing, my hand remained empty.

The image of a dream.

*Outside
darkness,
voices.*

In the neighborhood, a cat died. Elem Ryschon went to the funeral.

He told me about it; from a distance, I followed secretly.

The dead cat lay calmly on the doorstep. Shaggy funeral guests sat around it in a semicircle and, with thin, high voices, sang mournful songs.

The mewing hymn drifted out over the countryside.

Those are not really blind dogs.

The first fog.

Bearded old men under chestnut trees. New-borns on their knees. In the fields, a huge army of soldiers of dry grass. Detachments of straw horses. A general carved out of wood. Wind moving the fog. The figure in the cask quickly flies.

Chairs hurriedly run out of the houses, even tables stride across the village with dignity. Farmers singing in the tavern.

The figure in the cask quickly flew back. Accordions then flew in swarms to the east.

The Devil was parading about, roaring like a lion.

A shimmering automobile drove along the road, full of bat ears.

In the graveyard, a celebration. The sounds of a lute.

The fog was already thickening.

A cockcrow
in the day's din.

A wonderful rumor reached the village, even my ears. Apparently, Mr. Fuks catches his unicorns here in our region. He cuts off their horns and sells them as talismans. The horn of a unicorn brings good luck (as does the unicorn). It is also medicinal, it cures evil spells, jinxes, thin blood, aches of the head as well as those of the soul.

The nature of a unicorn is to act as a sentry. The unicorn is the silent protector of secret knowledge. A taciturn scholar. A wise visionary.

Mr. Fuks sells the unicorn, whose horn he has cut off, as an unusual breed of horse. These horses do not remain with their buyers long, however, for they bolt at the first chance.

This animal can only be caught with the help of a virgin.

Mr. Fuks has a daughter, Abigail.

And black roses blossomed. . .

First thing in the morning, to see Mr. Fuks.

I waited at the depot a long time before the train came. Then I took it to Jasini. The first person I asked in Jasini knew well the way to Mr. Fuks.

Mr. Fuks has a large store – modern. He himself sits behind the counter, behind the door at the end of the house. He is out of place amidst his property. He is black and wears old clothes, appearing to be a beggar.

He fixed his gaze on me at length and refused to reveal his hunting grounds.

Abigail Fuks brought food to the table. Both were kind to me.

After several hours, I managed to persuade them; they promised to take me along.

The voices of dogs
beyond the mountains.

Early morning, a dream chased me from bed. A difficult dream. The white body of a unicorn flying above me. I could not breathe, I was sweating.

The unicorn's horn pierced the sky. Stars poured swiftly to the ground like fruit blossoms.

The Fuks' awoke around five in the morning. I do not exactly know the time, there is no clock in the house.

We rode donkeys in the cool dew.

We came to a stop in mysterious, fragrant marshes. Fuks slouched with his finger at his lips. Abigail whispered something into her hands.

In those places, it was as if there were no sunrise. Quite the opposite, the darkness thickened.

Silently, we waited.

And finally, from the distance, a unicorn was approaching.

Abigail closed her eyes and, for some time, did not open them. Fuks tinkered with something by the donkey. I stared mutely at the magnificent animal, that dream come to life.

Then it happened. Abigail cried out. My unicorn ran off. We returned empty-handed. Surreptitiously, they looked at me. Perhaps I was the cause of the failure.

Then silently, it drizzled. The landscape went damp.

Blades of grass,
they are my little brothers.

Again, we awaken early and leave for the secret hunt of the unicorn. Abigail Fuks, me, and Moshe Fuks.

The Fuks' were not speaking to me and were glancing at one another. However, they neither said nor signaled that I should not follow them. They did not chase me out of the house.

The fog was dense. The donkeys faltered in silence through the meadow. We had been waiting for quite a while then Abigail whispered that she saw a unicorn. I strained my eyes in the fog. None came.

Again through the damp silence they glanced at one another.

I dismounted the donkey and bid them farewell. They did not stop me. They mumbled some words as good-bye.

I stayed at the »Traumentor« Inn. Traveling back by night to Voronskie Put' would have been pointless.

A large wave flooded
the earth.
Salty tears.

Unexpected events. Mr. Isaac Antan died. All of Voronskie Puť came to the funeral. Before the coffin passed a long procession of decorated horses. Certain signs were seen in the sky. Antan's stablehands went in their Sunday best. The rabbi gave a moving sermon. Even the famous Talmudist, Kuttenbrunz, came from Odessa. Other family friends also showed their pale faces.

And toward evening, into this hustle and bustle, an automobile, large and glittering, raised a cloud of dust. A Prague license plate. Chaim Finkel, the businessman, stepped out. He had shown up not suspecting the sad ceremony. He saw me among the people and joined me with an apologetic smile. He gave me a soft hand. He had come for his forgotten suitcase, he claimed.

The wailing sounds of the instruments were heard throughout the village.

Black cloth hung drooping from the windows.

Then everything was lost in a new wave of fog.

Bang on the window
the rattle of glass
will answer.

Businessman Finkel awoke in the morning later than I. He had calmly slept in my home, on a bed prepared by my hand. The house, which had once filled him with dread, did not rob him of sleep.

At the table we breakfasted on fish-paste.

Then, from the car, he brought in a package wrapped in fine paper. He smiled. He had a gift for me.

He insisted I immediately unwrap it. I removed from the package a beautifully embroidered blazon of Voronskie Put'. A black crow in flight. A crow wandering on a blue background of pure sky.

»I've taken a fancy to Voronskie,« Finkel said. »In my thoughts I always return.«

»What about the factory?« I asked.

»It's producing,« he said.

He did not speak about the land he had earlier wanted to purchase for Mr. Meisel.

He then sat over the fish-paste and was silent. I watched him and knew he would not be returning to Prague. One rich man has died, another is here. He is sitting at my table and will ever sit here.

A song sung
by shadowy mouths.
On the white wall, a figure.

Finkel left to visit Mumelschau the goat.

When he returned, he went out to visit the whole village.

When he then returned, he was the owner of the fields of the deceased Antan.

Elem Ryschon romped about in Finkel's automobile. He honked the horn and scratched the upholstery.

Everyone hid
in the dark cracks.

Fog. Severe rain in the afternoon.

Drops falling, constantly repeating the question, intrusively, callously. On my fingers I counted how many times I would not yet answer. Silence in my head, abandoned heart.

The wooden shutters on the houses beating their foreheads, grass quickly yellowing, closing its eyes. Stars flying up and down in the sky. They fell, bounced up from the earth, burning.

Ashy faces distorted mouths. Fingers clenched. Questions still prying, intrusively, callously. A muse ferociously pulling at Pegasus, urging him on with a whip.

Sizzling spume burning along the roads. Incandescent horseshoes in the fire. My soul bursting, empty. Words taking flight, floating away, elsewhere. Thieves quietly sneaking up, carrying off brick after brick.

OCTOBER 20

*I learn at night
from the trees
to understand
the shadows.*

Rain. On his meadow in silence stood
Mumelschau the goat running a hoof through his
long beard. With another, he dug Talmudic symbols
in the earth. It was dank, a chill was drifting in from
the forest. Chaim Finkel sat on a fallen tree trunk,
watching Mumelschau's symbols, smoking a cigarette,
drinking from a bottle.

I approached with Elem Ryschon. Hastily,
Mumelschau smudged the symbols. He pretended
that nothing had happened. He threw the stick into
the grass. We laughed at him, and then Ryschon went
off with him somewhere. Finkel put down the bottle,
slowly stood up, wearily embraced me. Above us a
seagull was circling. The clouds resembled human
figures.

Come, please,
I whisper
in my palms.

Chaim Finkel came. We stood a long time before the house. He leaned against the windowless wall of my house.

An horrific story. Some kind of evil spirit appears to him during the night, strolling through his head, tearing apart his mind. It began to visit his dreams in Prague.

Finkel suspected he had been bewitched by his former director, Mr. Meisel. He did not reveal why.

We then went to the tavern. Finkel wanted a nip to frighten off the night's visitor. Dilmatsch and Kornilov were sitting in the tavern; they advised us to go to Lesná, to the seer.

In the evening I wrote a letter to Mr. Murrer in Prague, with greetings also for Yom Kever.

OCTOBER 22

Fog is a voice,
voice of voices.

An immense fog has settled on Voronskie. The sound of an organ distinctly heard from heaven.

In Lesná, before the seer's hovel, a skeleton stood. We were startled, but the skeleton, wagging his finger, kindly invited us in, and it almost seemed as if his skull were smiling. Even from his eye sockets there glowed a kind of merry light. And so we entered. The seer sat with her head toward us, behind a large desk, the type found in the offices of high-ranking bureaucrats.

Actually, it looked like an office in the hovel. It was even possible to imagine the president's portrait on the wall. Bottles, vials, jars, and test tubes were piled in one corner. Various boxes, tools, and gadgets as well. The seer glanced at us, in her hand she held a large stuffed bird whose feathers she had just been painting with a brush. She asked what we wanted. Finkel told her about the demon in his head. She scratched her back for a while, put her large stuffed bird aside, and took out a notebook bound in canvas. Ceremonially, she sharpened a goose quill and wrote some words in ancient black ink from an ornate bottle.

She wrote for a long time. Every so often the skeleton looked in on us through the door and lit up his eye sockets.

The seer gave Finkel the inscribed paper and said, as in fairy tales – »Read it at home.« Then she charged five crowns for the advice, smiled at us, told us to not be afraid, that although she is selling rabbits in a sack, they are fresh.

Then she asked the skeleton, whom she called Chaimko, to see us off. He accompanied us a large part of the way, until he noiselessly parted with a deferential bow.

Are you not the moon,
you have such a white face.
I saw you behind the hill
and you fled.

I read through bulky old books with the rabbi. The rabbi blew the dust off their spines.

Unicorns reveal themselves in dreams. In the rabbi's books, we discovered the ancient homeland of these animals.

Organ music from the heavens.

They have delicate arms,
they will take you in hand.

Chaim Finkel came to divulge what the seer from Lesná at Pluzhno had advised. He was to acquire a glass bottle with a cork. Precisely at noon, he was to shut himself into a small, green chest and with a magic incantation summon his torturer. In the small space of the chest the demon would succumb to anxiety, look for a way to escape, and surely climb into the bottle, which then must be quickly sealed.

We were surprised by the silliness of the advice. But we did not lose faith in it. Finkel went out to the village to find a small green chest into which he could climb with his bottle.

The dogs barked and barked.

Above the village in the fog the organ tones played on.

I shall stroke the snake's body,
I shall hear the snakes' voices.

It was cozy at my table. Finkel sat with me, his head was drooping, he was falling asleep. The demon in the bottle shot red lightening from a niche in the wall.

Then Chaim Finkel straightened up and said: »Do you hear that noise, that laughter and clinking of glasses?« I listened to those sounds. Merry voices, the stir of an animated celebration resounded beneath the floor.

»Yes,« I said. »It's a fete. There's one there every day. You've never heard it, you didn't hear it yesterday?« He stared and shook his head. »I've never heard a party in your cellar.«

We went down to the cellar and I warned Finkel not to be frightened. He held onto me tightly. There was only a damp chill in the cellar. The celebration takes place further down, where no stairs lead. They carouse there every day, every day I can clearly hear them, they are Ghouls.

Outside in the fog, the organ continued to play from the sky.

A song of my own lips
will awaken me from a dream.

The rabbi pointed out to me the organ music from heaven. He looked at length in the direction whence it came. The fog, however, allowed nothing to be seen.

Then, in the fog, it rained. The rabbi stood amidst the elements. He remained completely dry. Around him, everything soaked through.

Dilmatsch joined us with a violin. He quietly accompanied the mysterious organ. He played according to sheet music that he said he had found in an orchard on the edge of the village. It probably fell there from the heavenly musician.

A great, colorful bird perched on the tree in front of my house.

Night wanderings in darkness,
a clamped throat anxious.
A bony hand.

The fog dissipated. The whole village ran to the square, gazing upward. Small angels sat in the sky, dramatically playing an organ. Kornilov was the first to wave, then we all waved at them. And the angels waved and called to us.

Then the dog of innkeeper Bem suddenly ascended to the clouds, barking, dispelling the angels, sinner.

We went sadly home. Bem did not speak to the dog, he tied him to a chain and punished him severely.

The rabbi smiled, soothed the old dog, eased his punishment. Then at night, unseen, he allegedly played tarots with him.

DECEMBER 5

*Tears brought
to my eyes by
the creaking of keys.*

Snow fell. I ran off to the white countryside. Elem
Ryschon ran at my heels, somersaulting grandly. We
were happy. It was cold. Pearls pouring out of tattered
sacks. Patches rotting in the country. Trees strumming
themselves. Lutes in the house windows. Stars
glittering in the clouds. A handful of silver in my
pockets.

Drying marzipan,
a kiss of snow.

    The forests doubled up, huddling together in coats. It was blowing sharply. Needle after needle stinging, sabers glistening, the army of snow dragging their standards. Everything slouched, slept. The countryside was like a spider's web, on the crossroads stood a table, jugs of milk upon it. By it a child, a red rose in hand. A red rose in the midst of the snow. I peeped into the windows at the people.

Then I ran farther.

No peace.

Flowered feather beds
in the country lay,
cushions starchy.
A procession of white geese.

Enveloped by the whiteness of winter. Blinded by the idea of the most radiant whiteness, dazzled by the manes of white unicorns, I am leaving.

Far away, away from the Voronskie region.

From a dream to a dream.

. . . A letter written in the scratchy writing of a cat's paw came by post. Elem Ryschon is inviting me to Voronskie. I bought a travel bag of the best pigskin from Jan Roller's.

And then, when I arrived at Voronskie Puť, greeting me, to my pleasant surprise, was not only Elem Ryschon, but the old Gypsy, the gendarme, the rabbi, the miller, and other local personalities. They all accompanied me up to Pinke's house. There, they gave me the key.

Ewald Murrer

Ewald Murrer was born in 1964, in Prague. After finishing his studies in 1985, he worked as a gardener at the President's Office at Prague Castle until 1990. In 1991, he received a stipendium from the Czech Literary Fund, and, in 1992, he initiated the literary journal *Iniciály*, of which he was editor-in-chief until 1994. Since that time, he has served as editor of Mladá Fronta publishers and Radio Echo. Besides the *Diary of Mr. Pinke*, he has had two collections of poetry published: *Fog Behind the Walls (Mlha za zdí*, 1992) and *Honor for a Lost War (Vyznamenání za prohranou válku*, 1992). He has also appeared in numerous anthologies including *Child of Europe* (Penguin Books, London, 1990), and has three further collections of poetry and stories being prepared for publication. He is currently working on his first novel.

Ewald Murrer
The Diary of Mr. Pinke

translated by Alicie Pišťková

Twisted Spoon Press
P.O. Box 21 – Preslova 12
150 21 Prague 5, Czech Republic

Editor Howard Sidenberg
Illustrations by Fedele Spadafora and Helena Vlčnovská

Typeset in Janson
Printed on Munken Print
Printed by PB Tisk, Rožmitálská 132, 261 02 Příbram VI
Czech Republic

First edition of 850 copies

ISBN: 80-90-1257-4-3

Prague, 1995